# OVERHEARING HISTORY

## The First in the Revolutionary Saratoga Story Series

WRITTEN BY
ANNE CLOTHIER

ILLUSTRATED BY
ALEX PORTAL

**Copyright © 2025 by Campaign for Saratoga 250, Inc.**

All rights reserved.

No part of this publication may be reproduced, stored in a retrieval system, or transmitted in any form or by any means—electronic, mechanical, photocopying, recording, or otherwise—without the prior written permission of the publisher, except in the case of brief quotations used in reviews or scholarly works.

**First published in 2025 by:** Campaign for Saratoga 250, Inc., 125 High Rock Avenue, Suite 210, Saratoga Springs, NY 12866

**Trademark Notice:** Saratoga 250 marks, including taglines, may be trademarks or registered trademarks. They are used in this publication strictly for identification and informational purposes, without intent to infringe.

**Image Locations:** Saratoga National Historical Park, The Farmers' Museum & Old Sturbridge Village

**Printed in the United States of America.**

**ISBN:** 979-8-218-68540-9

# This book belongs to:

_____

We gratefully acknowledge the assistance and support of:
Saratoga County and the Saratoga 250 Commission
Saratoga National Historical Park
The Campaign for Saratoga 250, Inc., *a 501(c)3 corporation*

# Introduction

In "Overhearing History: A Revolutionary Saratoga Story," step into the world of Nathaniel, a 12-year-old boy in 1775 Saratoga District, Albany County. Living in his parents' tavern and inn, Nathaniel overhears heated conversations that echo the rising tensions at the onset of what becomes the American Revolution. From Loyalists defending British rule, to Patriots demanding freedom, and enslaved servants questioning their rights, the diverse voices reveal a community at a crossroads. As debates over taxes, militias, and independence mount, Nathaniel witnesses influential voices in his life grappling with conflicting loyalties and the challenges of an emerging conflict.

This engaging historical fiction tale captures the uncertainty of a coming conflict in 1775 through a young child's eyes, drawing parallels to modern discussions on freedom, justice, and community. Perfect for young readers and history enthusiasts, this story invites reflection on what it means to live in a time of upheaval. Discussion prompts and keyword guides included to promote discussion with parents, family, teachers, and peers.

# Saratoga District 1775

# The year is 1775.

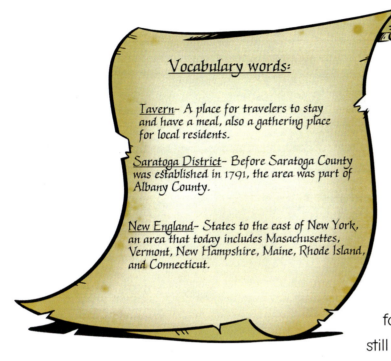

**Vocabulary words:**

<u>Tavern</u>- A place for travelers to stay and have a meal, also a gathering place for local residents.

<u>Saratoga District</u>- Before Saratoga County was established in 1791, the area was part of Albany County.

<u>New England</u>- States to the east of New York, an area that today includes Masachusettes, Vermont, New Hampshire, Maine, Rhode Island, and Connecticut.

Nathaniel is a 12-year-old boy living with his parents who are <u>tavern</u> keepers in the <u>Saratoga District</u> of Albany County. The area is full of good farmland, creeks and rivers to run mill waterwheels, and trees for building materials, yet still close to the more urban communities of Albany and Schenectady. Originally inhabited by indigenous groups including the Mohicans, Abenaki, and Mohawk people, the region is now facing rapid growth due to settlers arriving from eastern <u>New England</u> and Europe. Communities and town leaders communicate with each other through Committees of Correspondence, which share news, requests for independence, and organize to promote representation in the government. As Nathaniel goes about his day, he observes his neighbors and hears some of their conversations.

**Little does he know he's overhearing history in the making...**

> **Vocabulary words:**
>
> <u>Ale</u> – A type of beer that was frequently served at taverns in the 1700s.
>
> <u>Tarred and Feathered</u> – A form of punishment and torture in which hot pitch is pured on a person's skin and they are then covered in feathers. It is meant to be painful as well as embarrassing.
>
> <u>Ferry</u> – A way to cross a river using a raft pulled back and forth across water along a strong rope.
>
> <u>Tory & Loyalist</u> – These are terms for Americans who decided to remain loyal to England.

Nathaniel is milking his family's cow and overhears his parents talking softly outside the barn.

"Joseph, I'm worried," Nathaniel's mother says. "My father says he can't believe so many are rebelling against England. I've heard the men in the bar room. They shout about freedom and rights."

"Calm yourself, Emma," his father replies. "You know how they get when they have had too many pints of <u>ale</u>. It's all talk."

"It may be all talk now, but they seem to be getting angrier and angrier," his mother argued. "And the news out of Boston shows that a mob of angry men can do terrible things! First, they dumped all that tea, and now they've <u>tarred and feathered</u> a man they did not agree with!"

"The destruction of property is concerning, and the harming of people is even worse," his father answers. "But that is so far away, and in a place known for their tempers."

"But people here echo those sentiments," Emma continues. "My father has been threatened at the <u>ferry</u> and called a 'Rank <u>Tory</u>.'"

"I would like to believe that our neighbors are far more civil," Joseph says. "But do watch yourself and be careful about what you say. I hope your father knows well enough to stay quiet and hopefully the talk of him being a <u>loyalist</u> will cease."

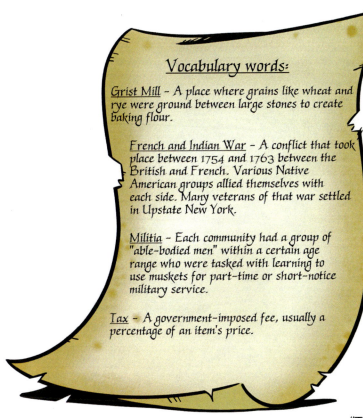

**Vocabulary words:**

<u>Grist Mill</u> - A place where grains like wheat and rye were ground between large stones to create baking flour.

<u>French and Indian War</u> - A conflict that took place between 1754 and 1763 between the British and French. Various Native American groups allied themselves with each side. Many veterans of that war settled in Upstate New York.

<u>Militia</u> - Each community had a group of "able-bodied men" within a certain age range who were tasked with learning to use muskets for part-time or short-notice military service.

<u>Tax</u> - A government-imposed fee, usually a percentage of an item's price.

After finishing his chores, Nathaniel goes to the <u>grist mill</u> and helps the miller, Mr. Clarke, fill cloth sacks with grain. Mr. Clarke uses a cane due to an old wound he received from fighting for the British in the <u>French and Indian War</u>.

"Nathaniel, you are such a good help here at the mill," Mr. Clarke says. "You're picking up the skills so well."

"Thank you, sir," Nathaniel replies.

"You're faster than that last boy who worked here. He was careless and couldn't wait to go meet with his friends. Now look at him! Off running with those rabble boys he met from the <u>militia</u> and raging against England! It's only fair that we pay something for the protection England has provided to us. After all the years I spent with the British Army, and the blood I shed, I know that it costs something to keep soldiers at the ready! Now they protest the <u>taxes</u> that pay for that army. No one complained when the British soldiers were here protecting our farms and settlements!"

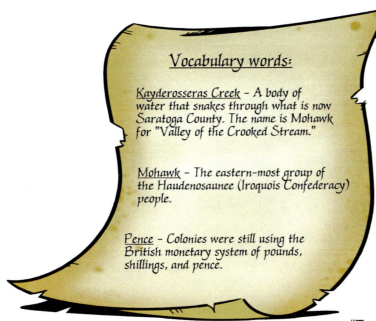

**Vocabulary words:**

<u>Kayderosseras Creek</u> - A body of water that snakes through what is now Saratoga County. The name is Mohawk for "Valley of the Crooked Stream."

<u>Mohawk</u> - The eastern-most group of the Haudenosaunee (Iroquois Confederacy) people.

<u>Pence</u> - Colonies were still using the British monetary system of pounds, shillings, and pence.

As Nathaniel sits down to eat his noon meal near the mill along the <u>Kayderosseras Creek</u>, he sees Mrs. Clarke talking with Hester, a <u>Mohawk</u> woman who weaves and sells baskets.

"How much for the small round one, Hester," Mrs. Clarke asks.

"Ten <u>pence</u>," Hester answers.

"Where are you living now," Mrs. Clarke inquires.

"Out west of the fork in the road," the old Mohawk woman replies. "My grandmother's grandmother knew these fields and forests. But every few months a new farmstead is built and they start clearing more and more trees. Last week a cow wandered into my garden and ate all of my beans and peas."

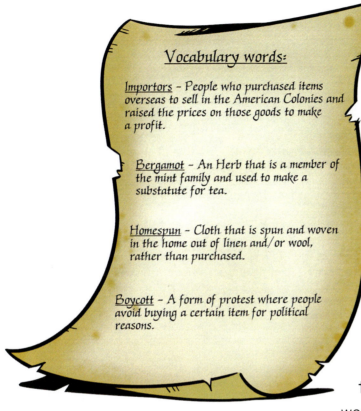

**Vocabulary words:**

<u>Importors</u> - People who purchased items overseas to sell in the American Colonies and raised the prices on those goods to make a profit.

<u>Bergamot</u> - An Herb that is a member of the mint family and used to make a substatute for tea.

<u>Homespun</u> - Cloth that is spun and woven in the home out of linen and/or wool, rather than purchased.

<u>Boycott</u> - A form of protest where people avoid buying a certain item for political reasons.

Nathaniel stops at a neighbor's house to pick up a packet of pins and some thread that his mother asked him to get on the way home. He sees two women sitting on the porch.

"The cost of tea is outlandish," one of the women exclaims.

"I still don't know why you haven't switched over to raspberry leaf," the other woman responds.

"It is as good as any other tea, and much more wholesome in the end. And it keeps the money out of the hands of those <u>importers</u>!"

"I know. I find <u>bergamot</u> to be tolerable. But I do miss proper tea," the first woman answers.

"I think we all do, one way or another," the second woman says. "What I dread is finding new sources for cloth. <u>Homespun</u> has its place in the home, but I prefer good English wool and linen for my garments. Some are talking about <u>boycotting</u> all goods imported from England."

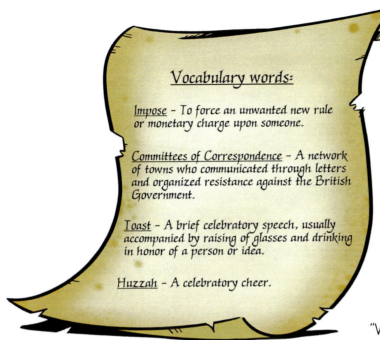

**Vocabulary words:**

<u>Impose</u> – To force an unwanted new rule or monetary charge upon someone.

<u>Committees of Correspondence</u> – A network of towns who communicated through letters and organized resistance against the British Government.

<u>Toast</u> – A brief celebratory speech, usually accompanied by raising of glasses and drinking in honor of a person or idea.

<u>Huzzah</u> – A celebratory cheer.

Back at his parent's tavern later that evening, Nathaniel brings another plate of bread out into the bar room. The room is full of people, laughter, and conversation. Nathaniel's neighbor, Mr. Gordon stands up. His booming voice projects out into the room and a hush falls over the tavern patrons.

"We are done being the subjects of a country across the ocean," Mr. Gordon yells. "Men who sit thousands of miles away have no right to tell us what we can and cannot do! They <u>impose</u> tax upon tax, while we are given no say! It is time to unite and govern ourselves!

The <u>Committees of Correspondence</u> are working to unify our towns and forge a nation of united Colonies! No longer will we toast to the Mother Country, but <u>toast</u> to our rights!"

"<u>Huzzah</u>!" the other patrons cry out in agreement.

"A toast to all true Patriots throughout the world," Mr. Gordon continues.

**"Huzzah!"**

"To our militia who is ready to heed the call of duty!"

**"Huzzah!"**

"To the rights of mankind in every quarter of the globe!"

**"Huzzah!"**

Vocabulary words:

<u>Punch</u> – A drink made with fruit, sugar, and alcohol and drank out of a large bowl.

<u>Sugar Cones</u> – Sugar was sold in solid cones wrapped in blue paper in the 1700s.

<u>Enslaved Servant</u> – A person who was said to be legally owned by another person and forced to work without pay.

<u>Turnips</u> – A root vegetable that can be easily stored over the winter.

Bowl after bowl of <u>punch</u> is being passed around at the tavern. Nathaniel is sent to borrow some sugar from Mrs. Gordon down the road. He knocks on the door. Mrs. Gordon greets him, sends him to the kitchen, and tells him to take a blue paper-wrapped <u>sugar cone</u> off the shelf. There he sees Ann and Jacob, two of the <u>enslaved servants</u>. They sit by the fire, peeling <u>turnips</u> and chatting quietly. They do not hear Nathaniel enter.

"Mr. Gordon keeps talking of freedom and the rights of mankind," Ann says. "Yet he owns us. What rights do we have?"

"If anything were to happen to him, we'd likely be sold," Jacob replies. "To where? To whom?"

"When Mr. Andrews died, Betty the cook was sold to one person, and her son James sold to someone else! He is only six," Ann continues. "I don't know that she's yet found out where he ended up."

Nathaniel prepares for bed. His parents come in to wish him a good night. He takes this opportunity to share some of what he has heard throughout his long day.

"These are indeed challenging times. And I fear that we will face more, and soon," his father says. "It is like hearing a distant thunderstorm rolling in, as happened last week. We can hear it and we know it's coming. The best we can do is prepare, keep our wits about us, and hope for the best."

"Mr. Gordon and Mr. Clarke are both good men and have done good things for our family," Nathaniel poses. "But they say such opposing things and they don't seem to like each other. What will happen between them? And what about grandfather? I don't like people calling him names."

"To be honest, Nathaniel, I don't know," his mother admits. "Try to rest your mind and we can talk more in the morning."

And with that, Nathaniel closed his eyes and dreamed of the future.

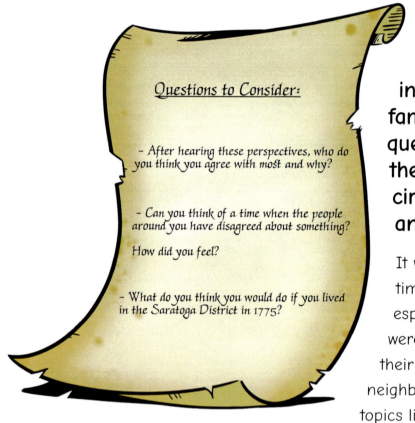

*Questions to Consider:*

- *After hearing these perspectives, who do you think you agree with most and why?*

- *Can you think of a time when the people around you have disagreed about something? How did you feel?*

- *What do you think you would do if you lived in the Saratoga District in 1775?*

**1775 was a pivotal year when many individuals and families began questioning their own circumstances and loyalties.**

It was a confusing time for everyone, especially kids who were witnessing their families and neighbors discuss topics like power, leadership, citizenship, and money. Sometimes these conversations led to debates and arguments.

Thinking about Nathaniel's experiences, what are some of the parallels between the people who lived 250 years ago and those of us who live today in the 21st century?

# Meet the Author

**Anne Clothier** has always loved history. She grew up on her family's 200-year-old farm in northern Saratoga County, where old stories and traditions were part of everyday life. Today, Anne brings history to life by teaching kids and adults what it was like to live in the 1700s — especially the stories of Loyalists during the American Revolution.

She loves learning about women's history, old-fashioned clothing and fabrics, and how people used to take care of their health. Anne studied history in college and learned even more at the Cooperstown Graduate Program, where she worked at cool places like The Farmers' Museum and the Fenimore Art Museum.

Before becoming the Assistant to the Saratoga County Historian, Anne spent over 10 years helping people explore the past as Director of Education at the Brookside Museum.

# Meet the Illustrator

**Alex Portal** grew up in Pennsylvania and loved cartoons and comic books from the very start. As a kid, he spent hours drawing on just about anything he could find — notebooks, napkins, even the back of his homework!

Today, Alex is a cartoonist who creates pictures for all kinds of books. He's worked with lots of authors, including on the "But Nana..."Deadwood adventure series and "Grandpa's White Cane," which is even in the Library of Congress!

Alex is a proud member of the National Cartoonists Society and has won awards for his funny and creative drawings. He now lives in Queensbury, New York, with his wife. Alex is excited to bring Overhearing History: A Revolutionary Saratoga Story to life with his illustrations — combining his love of drawing and history all in one book.

# Want to Learn More?

Discover more about Saratoga's Revolutionary heritage—including educational videos, local events, and real stories from the 1700s.

## visit Saratoga250.com

Made in United States
North Haven, CT
16 July 2025

70755971R00015